HAL•LEONARD

JAZZ PLAY-ALONG

Book and CD for B♭, E♭, C and Bass Clef Instruments

volume 137

Arranged and Produced by Mark Taylor and Jim Roberts

Wes Montgomery

10 Favorite Tunes

Cover photo © Rolf Ambor/CTSIMAGES.COM

ISBN 978-1-4234-9452-2

HAL•LEONARD CORPORATION

7777 W. BLUEMOUND RD. P.O. BOX 13819 MILWAUKEE, WI 53213

Visit Hal Leonard Online at
www.halleonard.com

WES MONTGOMERY

Volume 137

**Arranged and Produced by
Mark Taylor and Jim Roberts**

Featured Players:

Paul Murtha–Trumpet
John Desalme–Sax
Tony Nalker–Piano
Jim Roberts–Bass
Todd Harrison–Drums

**Recorded at Bias Studios, Springfield, Virginia
Bob Dawson, Engineer**

HOW TO USE THE CD:

Each song has <u>two</u> tracks:

1) Split Track/Melody

Woodwind, Brass Keyboard, and **Mallet Players** can use this track as a learning tool for melody style and inflection.

Bass Players can learn and perform with this track – remove the recorded bass track by turning down the volume on the LEFT channel.

Keyboard and **Guitar Players** can learn and perform with this track – remove the recorded piano part by turning down the volume on the RIGHT channel.

2) Full Stereo Track

Soloists or **Groups** can learn and perform with this accompaniment track with the RHYTHM SECTION only.

D NATURAL BLUES

BY JOHN L. (WES) MONTGOMERY

C VERSION

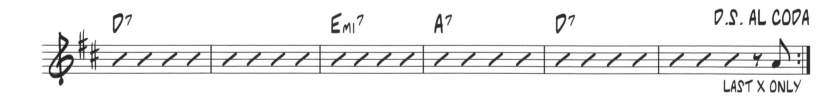

FRIED PIES

BY JOHN L. (WES) MONTGOMERY

CD
- **3** : SPLIT TRACK/MELODY
- **4** : FULL STEREO TRACK

C VERSION

FOUR ON SIX

BY JOHN L. (WES) MONTGOMERY

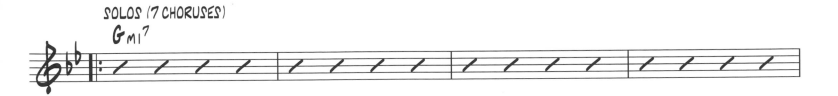

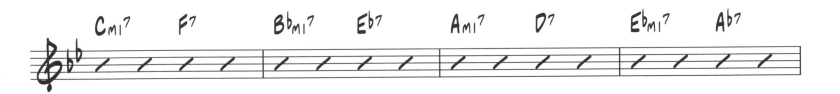

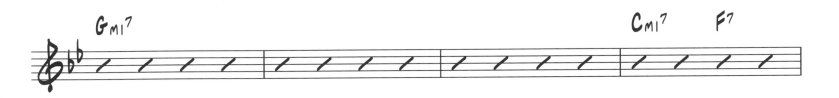

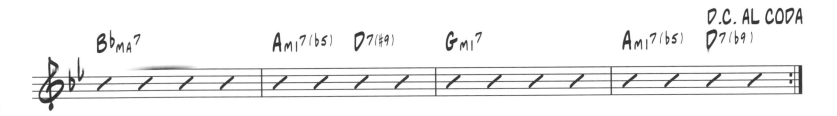

ROAD SONG

CD
7 : SPLIT TRACK/MELODY
8 : FULL STEREO TRACK

BY JOHN L. (WES) MONTGOMERY

C VERSION

Sundown

CD
9: SPLIT TRACK/MELODY
10: FULL STEREO TRACK

C VERSION

BY JOHN L. (WES) MONTGOMERY

SWITCHIN'

BY JOHN L. (WES) MONTGOMERY

CD
11 : SPLIT TRACK/MELODY
12 : FULL STEREO TRACK

C VERSION

WEST COAST BLUES

BY JOHN L. (WES) MONTGOMERY

C VERSION

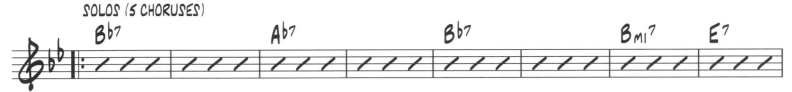

CD

13: SPLIT TRACK/MELODY
14: FULL STEREO TRACK

TEQUILA

BY CHUCK RIO

C VERSION

MEDIUM LATIN

CD

15 : SPLIT TRACK/MELODY
16 : FULL STEREO TRACK

TWISTED BLUES

BY JOHN L. (WES) MONTGOMERY

C VERSION

FAST SWING

TO CODA ✛

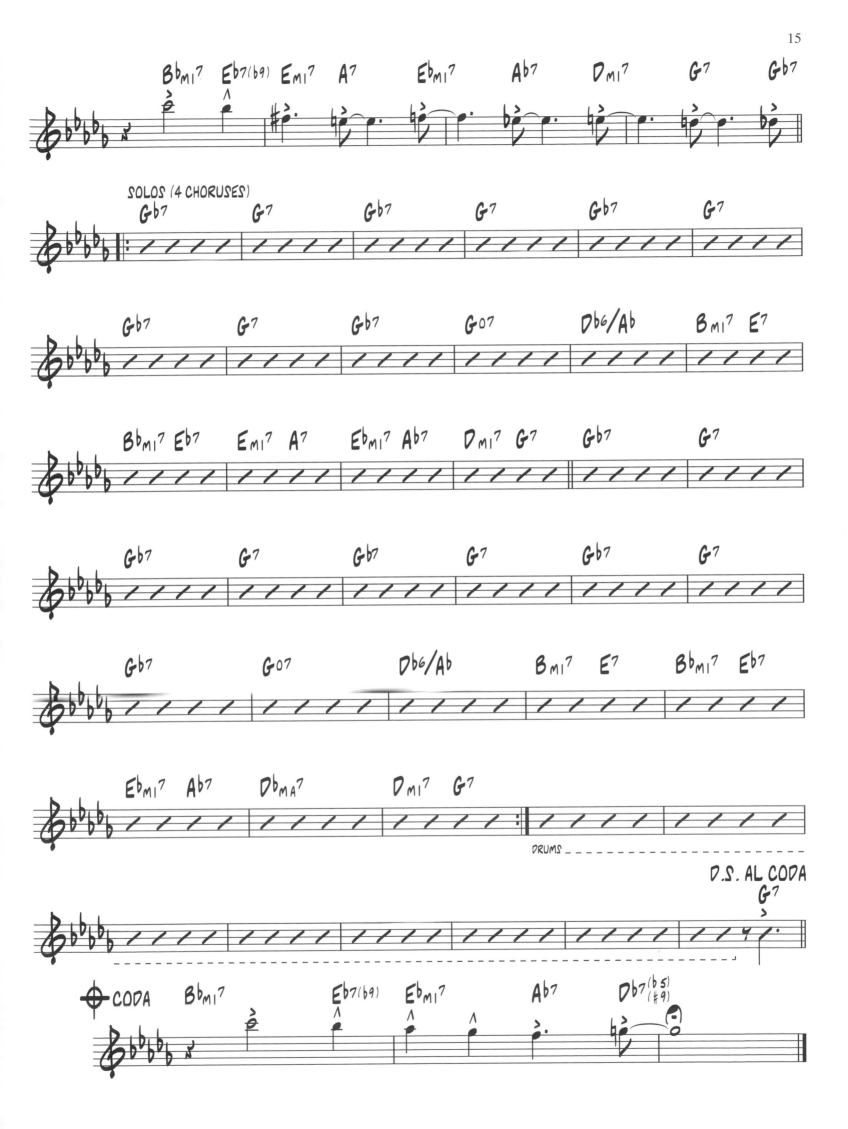

WINDY

CD
◆19: SPLIT TRACK/MELODY
◆20: FULL STEREO TRACK

WORDS AND MUSIC BY
RUTHANN FRIEDMAN

C VERSION

WINDY

CD
19 : SPLIT TRACK/MELODY
20 : FULL STEREO TRACK

WORDS AND MUSIC BY
RUTHANN FRIEDMAN

Bb VERSION

CD

1 : SPLIT TRACK/MELODY
2 : FULL STEREO TRACK

D NATURAL BLUES

BY JOHN L. (WES) MONTGOMERY

Bb VERSION

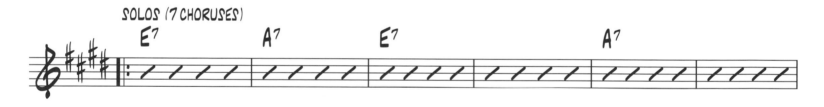
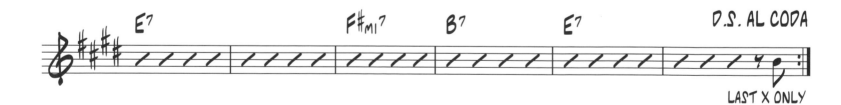

FRIED PIES

BY JOHN L. (WES) MONTGOMERY

CD
- **5** : SPLIT TRACK/MELODY
- **6** : FULL STEREO TRACK

Bb VERSION

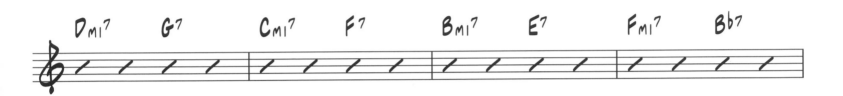

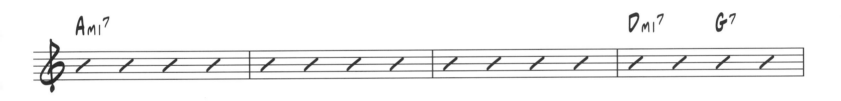

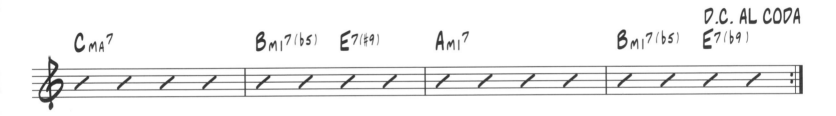

ROAD SONG

BY JOHN L. (WES) MONTGOMERY

Bb VERSION

Sundown

BY JOHN L. (WES) MONTGOMERY

CD
9 : SPLIT TRACK/MELODY
10 : FULL STEREO TRACK

Bb VERSION

Switchin'

CD
◆11: SPLIT TRACK/MELODY
◆12: FULL STEREO TRACK

BY JOHN L. (WES) MONTGOMERY

Bb VERSION

CD
17: SPLIT TRACK/MELODY
18: FULL STEREO TRACK

WEST COAST BLUES

BY JOHN L. (WES) MONTGOMERY

Bb VERSION

MEDIUM BLUES

CD

13 : SPLIT TRACK/MELODY
14 : FULL STEREO TRACK

TEQUILA

BY CHUCK RIO

Bb VERSION

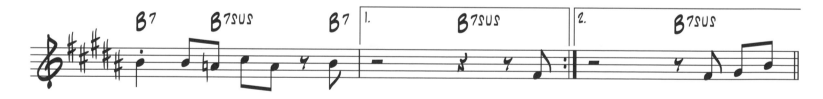

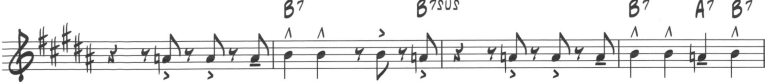

CD
15 : SPLIT TRACK/MELODY
16 : FULL STEREO TRACK

TWISTED BLUES

BY JOHN L. (WES) MONTGOMERY

Bb VERSION

CD

① : SPLIT TRACK/MELODY
② : FULL STEREO TRACK

D NATURAL BLUES

BY JOHN L. (WES) MONTGOMERY

Eb VERSION

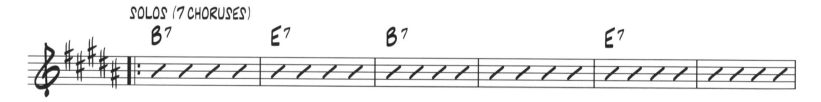

LAST X ONLY

FRIED PIES

BY JOHN L. (WES) MONTGOMERY

FOUR ON SIX

BY JOHN L. (WES) MONTGOMERY

Eb VERSION

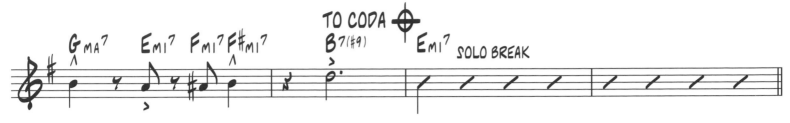

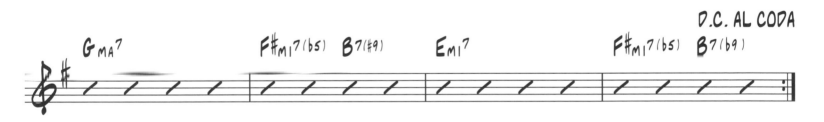

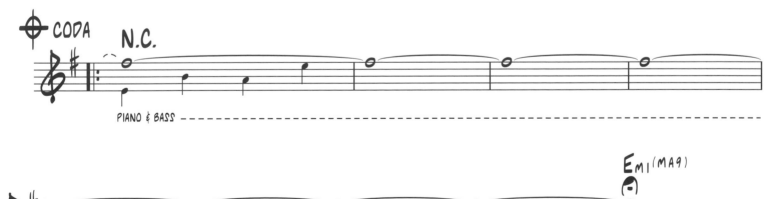

ROAD SONG

Sundown

CD
◆ **9** : SPLIT TRACK/MELODY
◆ **10** : FULL STEREO TRACK

Eb VERSION

BY JOHN L. (WES) MONTGOMERY

CD

17 : SPLIT TRACK/MELODY
18 : FULL STEREO TRACK

WEST COAST BLUES

BY JOHN L. (WES) MONTGOMERY

Eb VERSION

MEDIUM BLUES

SOLOS (5 CHORUSES)

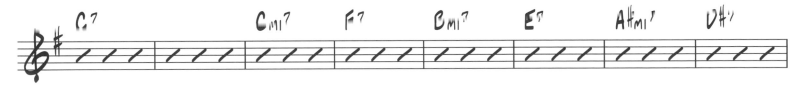

D.S. AL CODA

LAST X ONLY

TEQUILA

BY CHUCK RIO

Eb VERSION

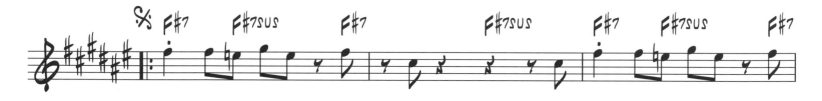

CD

15 : SPLIT TRACK/MELODY
16 : FULL STEREO TRACK

Twisted Blues

BY JOHN L. (WES) MONTGOMERY

Eb VERSION

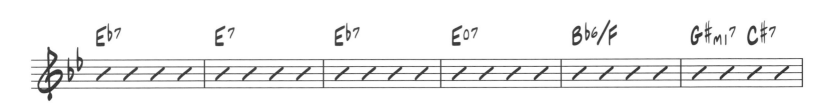

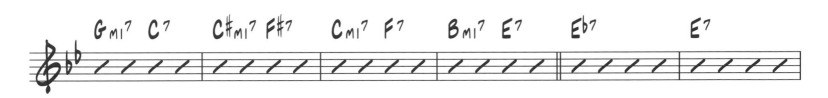

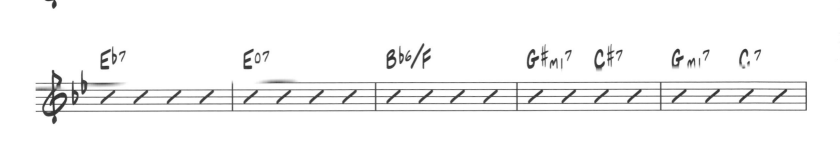

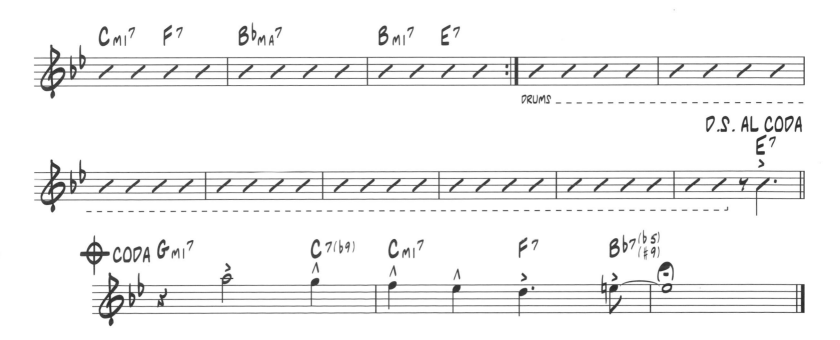

Windy

WORDS AND MUSIC BY
RUTHANN FRIEDMAN

WINDY

WORDS AND MUSIC BY
RUTHANN FRIEDMAN

CD
19 : SPLIT TRACK/MELODY
20 : FULL STEREO TRACK

𝄢: C VERSION

D NATURAL BLUES

BY JOHN L. (WES) MONTGOMERY

𝄢: C VERSION

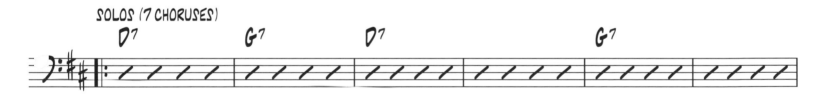

FRIED PIES

CD
5 : SPLIT TRACK/MELODY
6 : FULL STEREO TRACK

BY JOHN L. (WES) MONTGOMERY

𝄢: C VERSION

FOUR ON SIX

BY JOHN L. (WES) MONTGOMERY

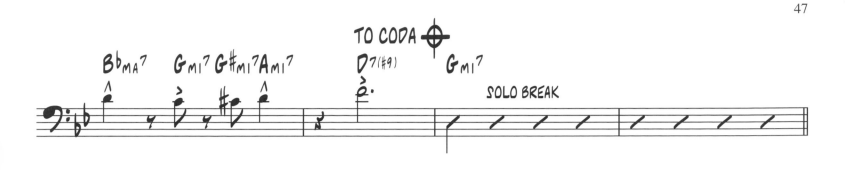

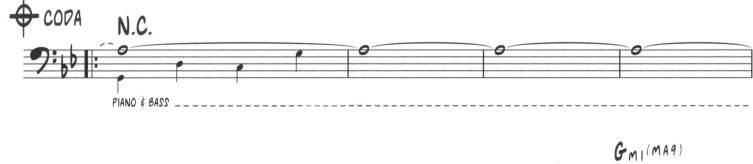

ROAD SONG

BY JOHN L. (WES) MONTGOMERY

Sundown

CD
9: SPLIT TRACK/MELODY
10: FULL STEREO TRACK

BY JOHN L. (WES) MONTGOMERY

SWITCHIN'

BY JOHN L. (WES) MONTGOMERY

WEST COAST BLUES

BY JOHN L. (WES) MONTGOMERY

CD
▲ : SPLIT TRACK/MELODY
18 : FULL STEREO TRACK

𝄢 C VERSION

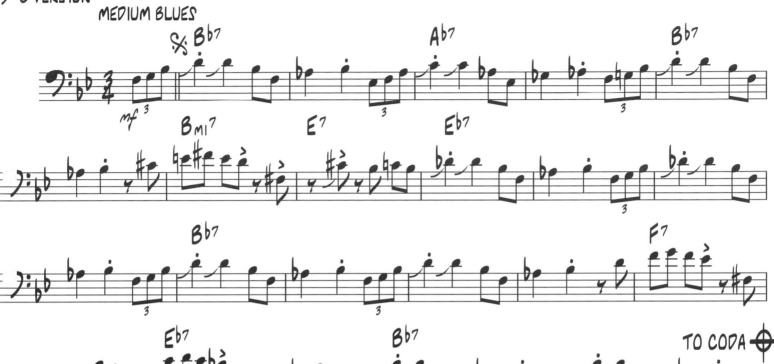

CD

13 : SPLIT TRACK/MELODY
14 : FULL STEREO TRACK

TEQUILA

BY CHUCK RIO

𝄢: C VERSION

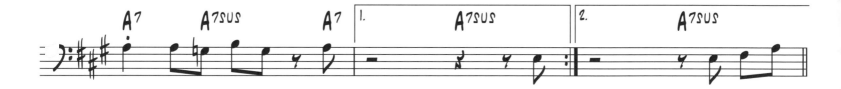

CD

◇15 : SPLIT TRACK/MELODY
◇16 : FULL STEREO TRACK

TWISTED BLUES

BY JOHN L. (WES) MONTGOMERY

𝄢: C VERSION

FAST SWING

TO CODA ⊕

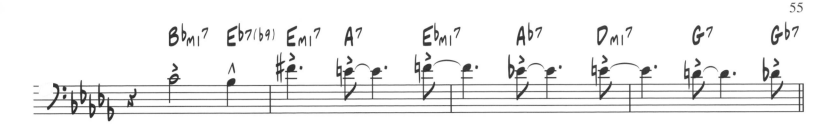

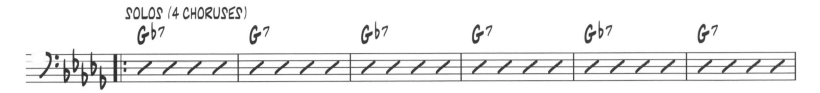

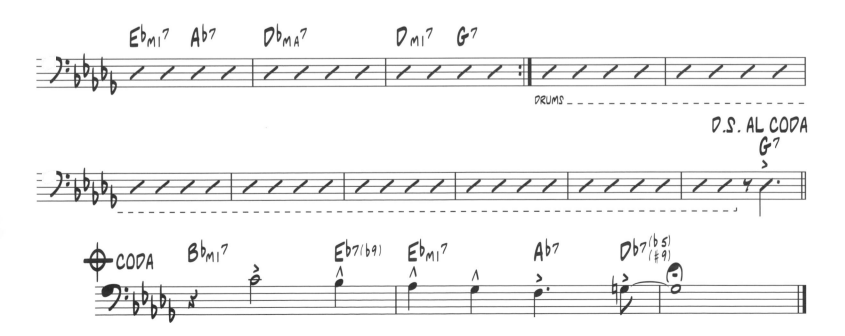

For use with all B-flat, E-flat, Bass Clef and C instruments, the Jazz Play-Along® Series is the ultimate learning tool for all jazz musicians. With musician-friendly lead sheets, melody cues, and other split-track choices on the included CD, these first-of-a-kind packages help you master improvisation while playing some of the greatest tunes of all time. FOR STUDY, each tune includes a split track with: melody cue with proper style and inflection • professional rhythm tracks • choruses for soloing • removable bass part • removable piano part. FOR PERFORMANCE, each tune also has: an additional full stereo accompaniment track (no melody) • additional choruses for soloing.